Destination ALASKA

Traveling Coloring Book:

Relax, Color and Take a Virtual Vacation

SensationalAlaska.com

TravelingColoringBook.com Series™
http://TravelingColoringBooks.com
http://Amazon.com/author/bruceoliver

BRUCE OLIVER

Travel Advisor & TV Host

Scent-Sational Travel & Food Resource Books™
Sensational Travel & Food Adult Coloring Books™

Axis Mundi Systems LLC dba Cruise with Bruce Enterprises

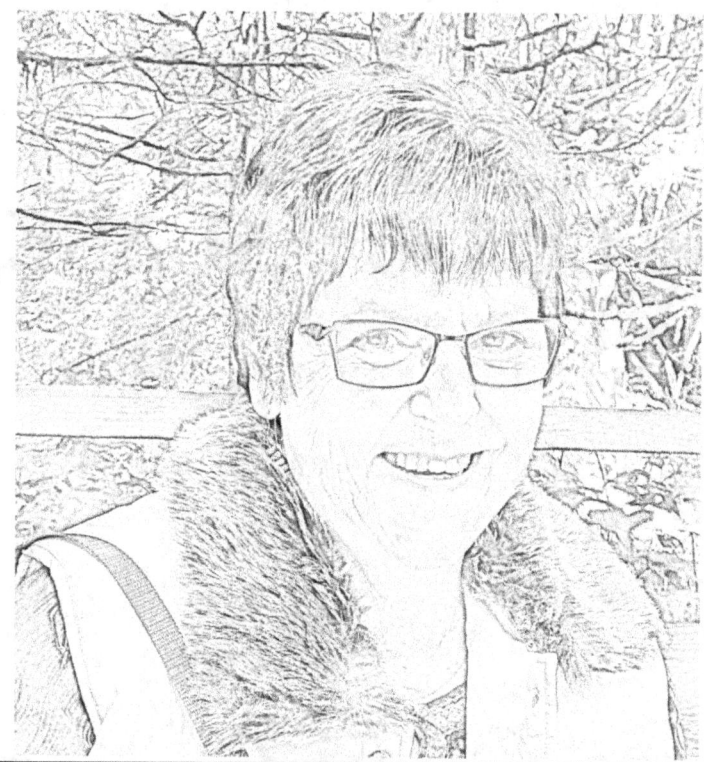

This Book Belongs to:

_____

- There are 30 pages for you to color as you take your Virtual Vacation.

- Each page has a description of where the photograph was taken to make the illustration.

- The illustration does not fill the page just in case you want to frame your masterpiece.

- You can order your next Destination Coloring Book by going to:

    http://TravelingColoringBooks.com

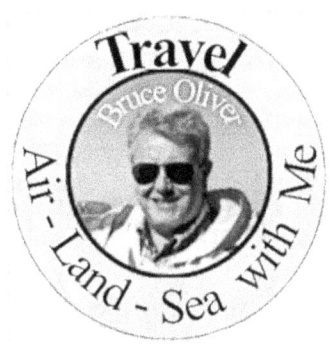

Bruce Oliver
Traveling Coloring Books

First edition 2017

The illustrations used throughout the book are the property of the author. Each illustration has been rendered from photographs taken by the author and turned into the line art used to color.

For more information about Bruce Oliver please visit the following websites:

http://ScratchAndSniffTravel.com
http://BruceOliverTV.com
http://ScentSationalAlaska.com
http://SensationalAlaska.com
http://Amazon.com/author/bruceoliver

Printed in the United States of America.
ISBN-13: 978-1-970029-06-2 (Vegas New Wave Media)
ISBN-10: 1-970029-06-4

Book your next trip or cruise by going to:
http://BruceOliverTV.com
and click on the CRUISE or VACATION menu choice at the top of the page

Bruce Oliver near the Hubbard Glacier — Alaska

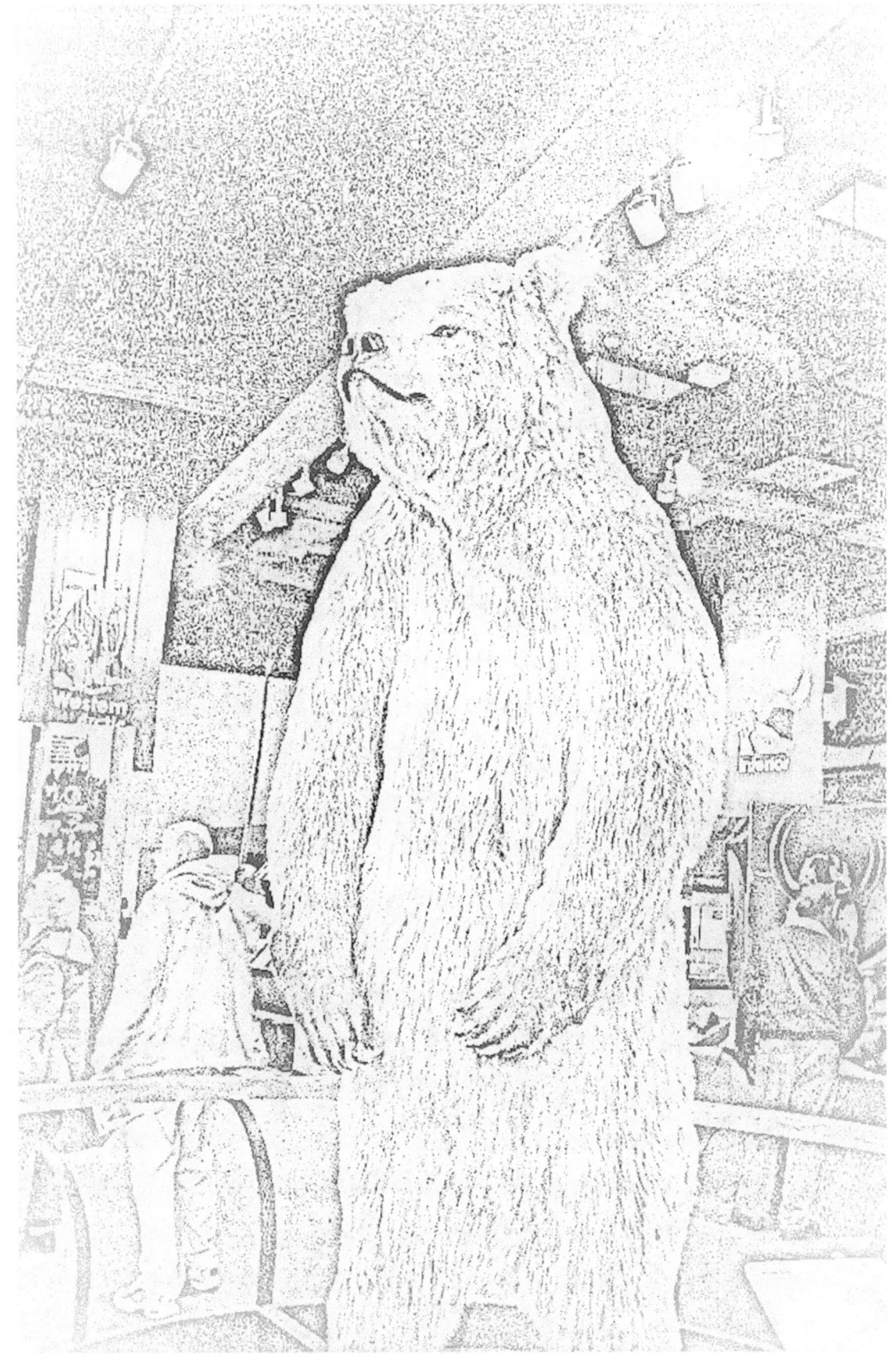

Kodiak Bear in the Fairbanks Natural History Museum — Fairbanks, Alaska

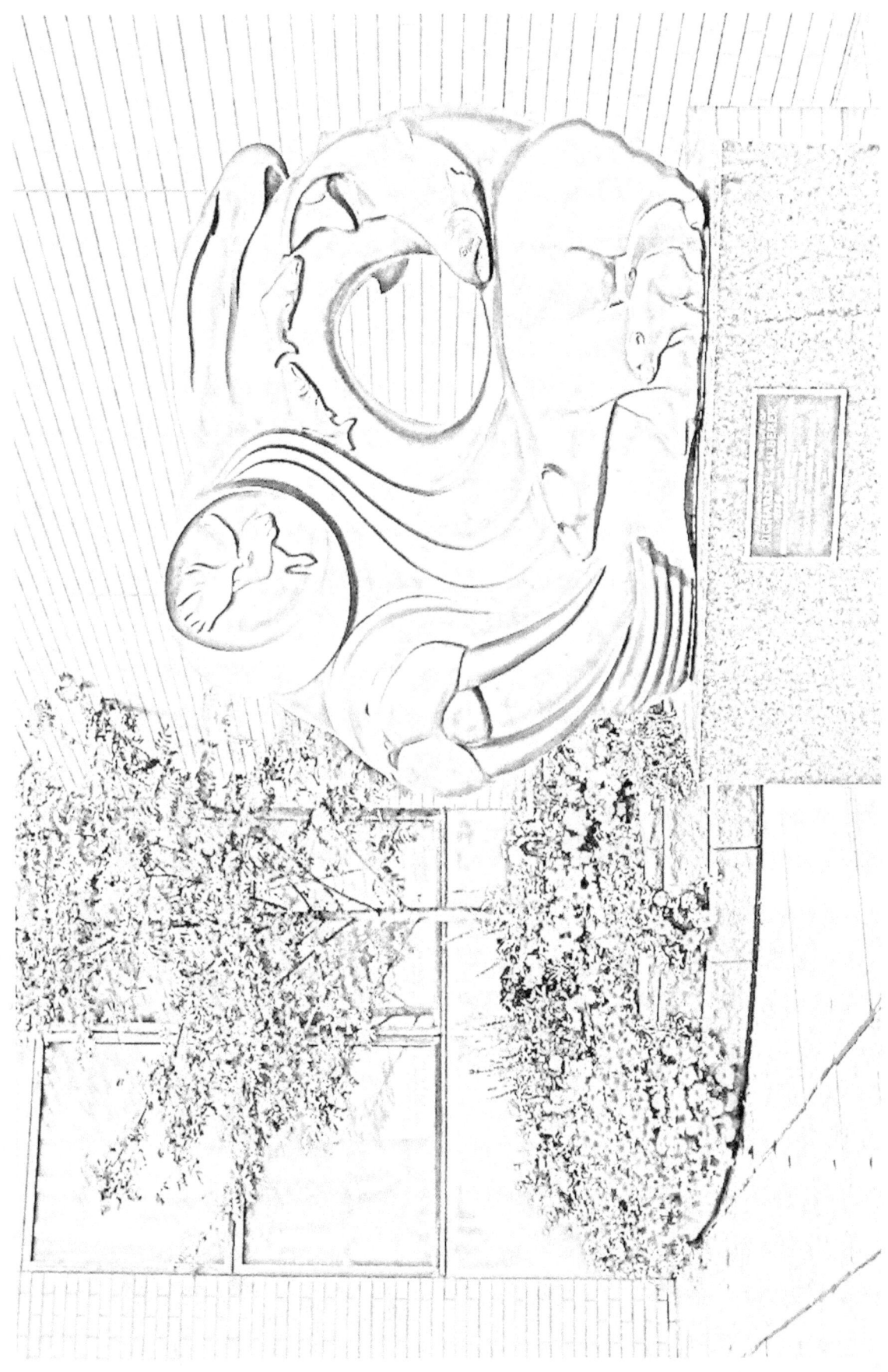

Bronze Sculpture — Anchorage, Alaska

Alaskan Railway — Denali, Alaska

Window on Creek Street — Ketchikan, Alaska

Alaskan Pipeline — North Fairbanks, Alaska

Paddle Boat — Fairbanks, Alaska

Chef at the Salmon Bake — Juneau, Alaska

Cabin on the River — Fairbanks, Alaska

Creek Street Creek — Ketchikan, Alaska

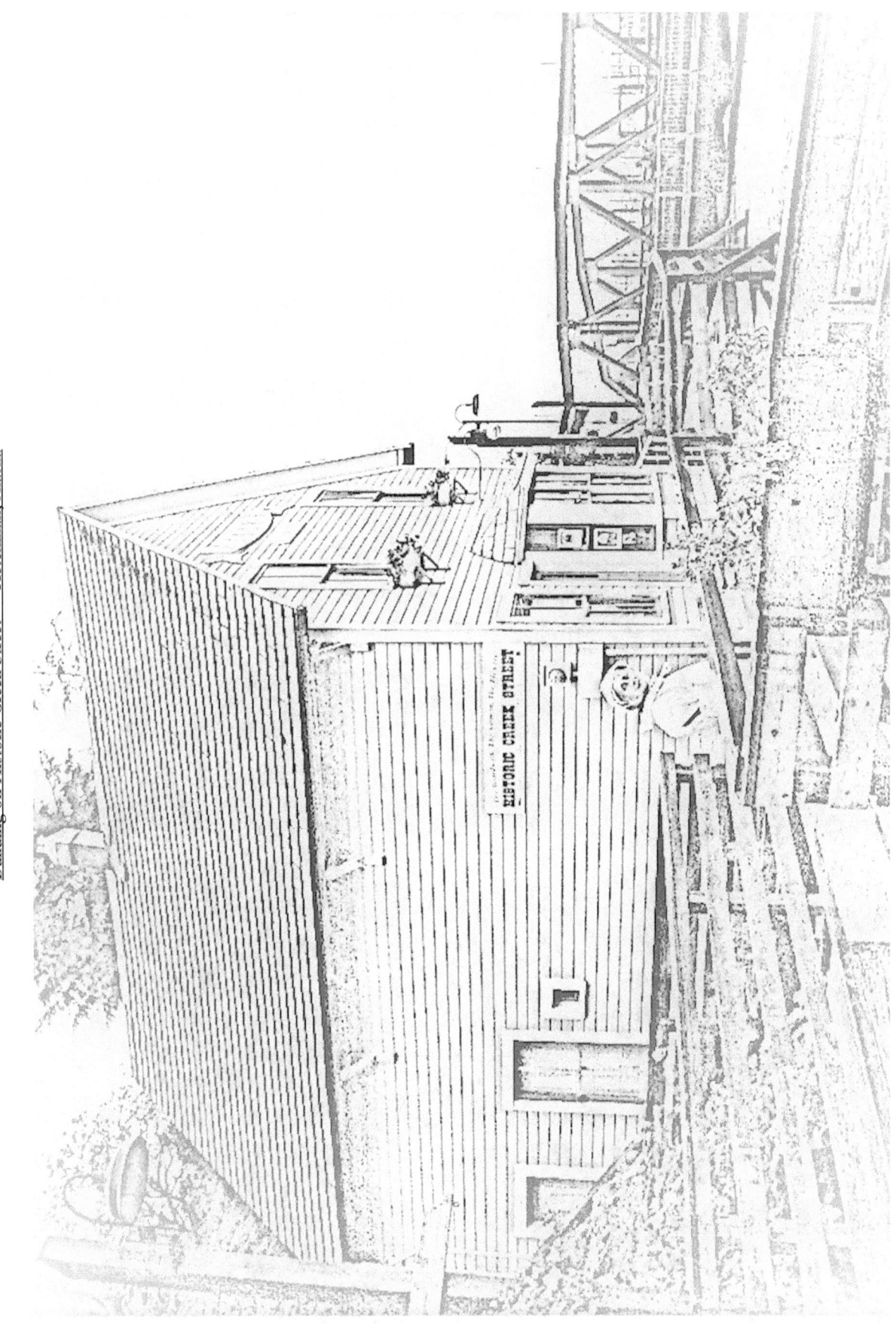

Building on Historic Creek Street — Ketchikan, Alaska

Moose — Denali National Park, Alaska

Mount Denali Range — Denali, Alaska

Paddle Boat Dock and Village — Fairbanks, Alaska

PIONEER HOTEL

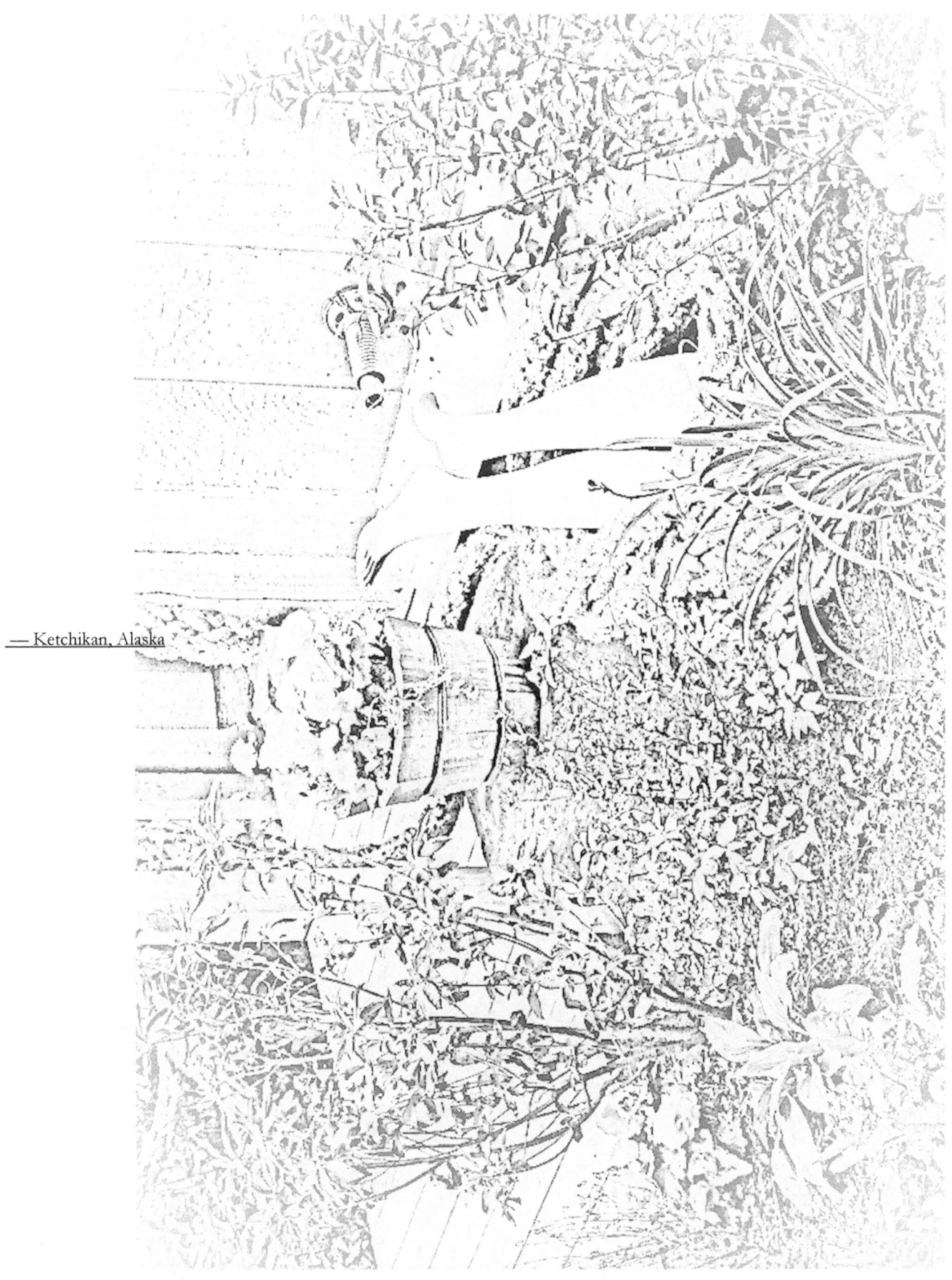

— Ketchikan, Alaska

Iditarod Headquarters — Outside of Anchorage, Alaska

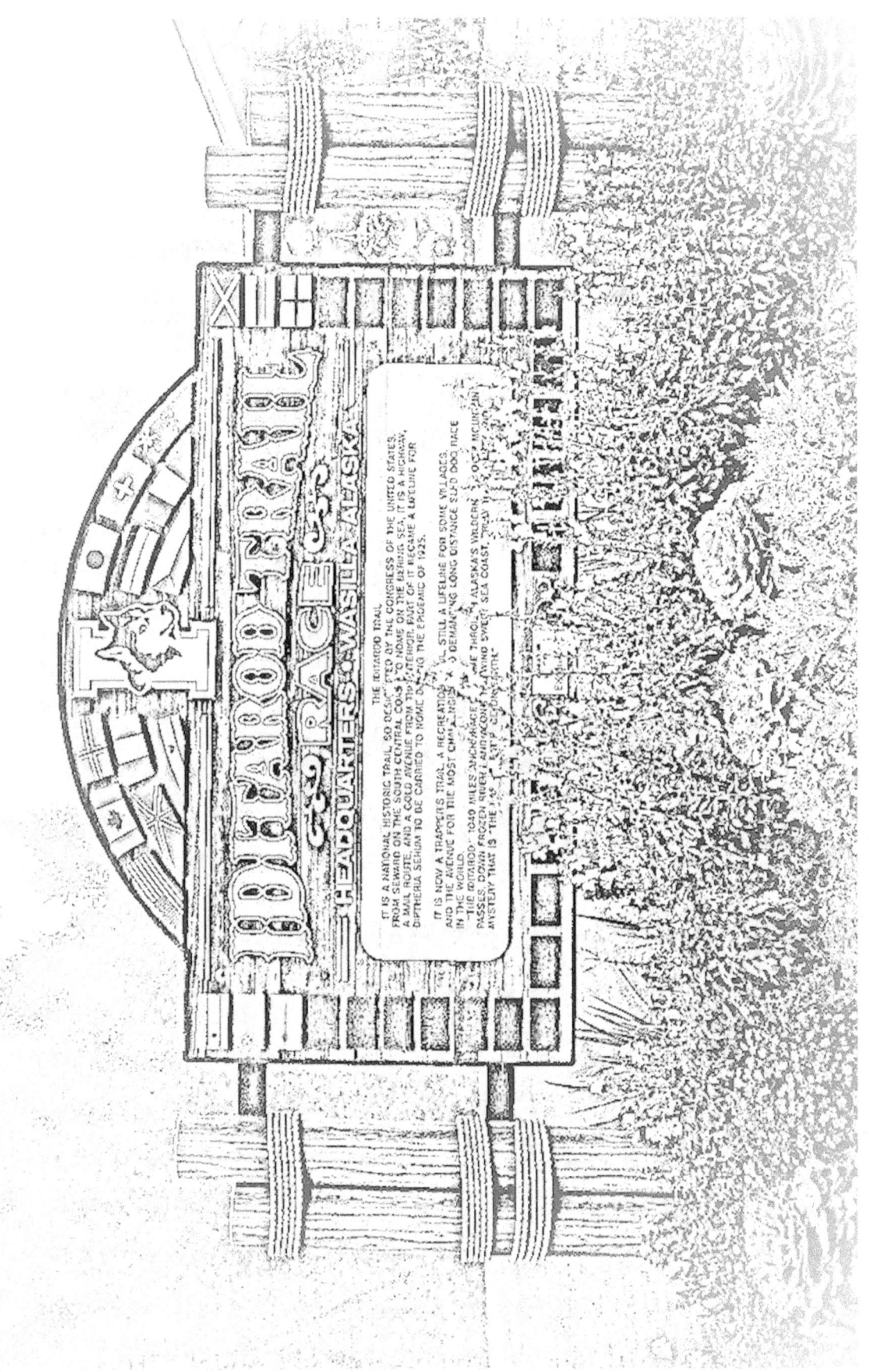

Red Dog Saloon — Juneau, Alaska

Ketchikan Center — Ketchikan, Alaska

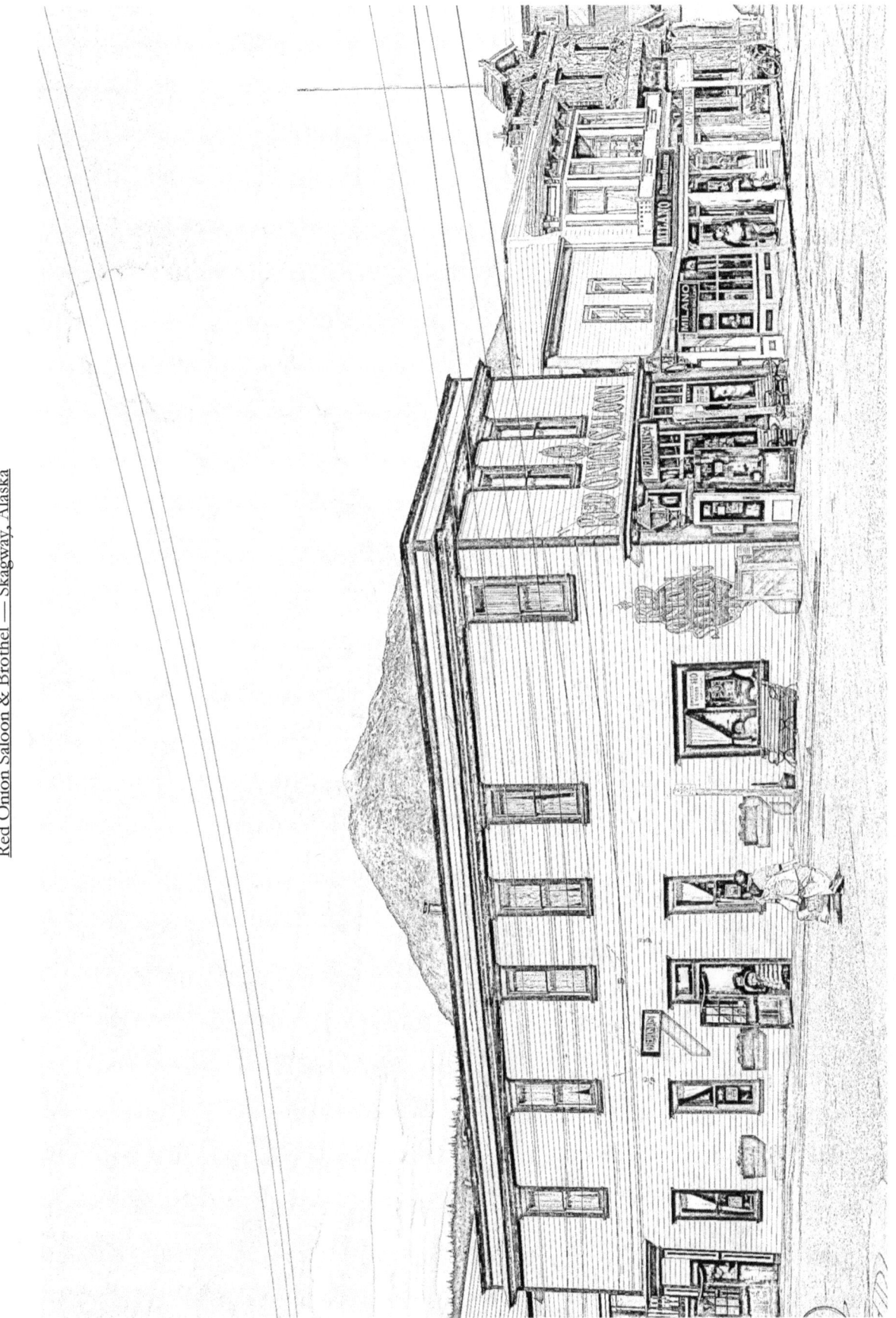

Red Onion Saloon & Brothel — Skagway, Alaska

White Pass Railway — Skagway, Alaska

Alaska Shoppe — Skagway, Alaska

Flowers — Denali, Alaska

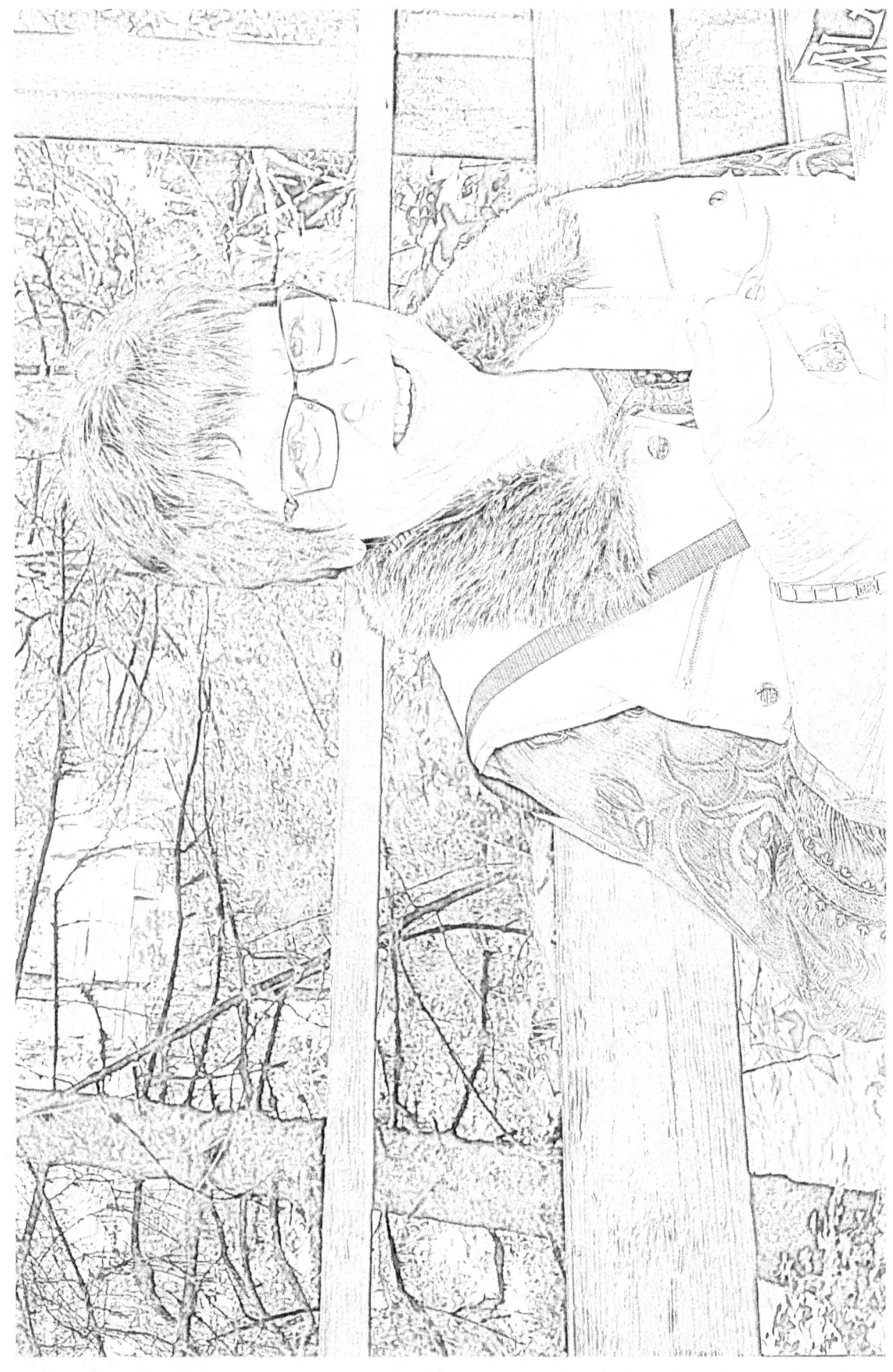

Sandy Eating Chowder — Juneau Salmon Bake, Alaska

Salmon — Creek Street Juneau, Alaska

Bruce Oliver trying on a Wolf Skin Cap — Creek Street Ketchikan, Alaska

Russian Block House — Sitka, Alaska

Garden, etc. — Skagway, Alaska

Bruce Oliver at the Salmon Bake — Juneau, Alaska

Flowers — Skagway, Alaska

Upside Down — Skagway, Alaska

www.ingramcontent.com/pod-product-compliance
Lightning Source LLC
Chambersburg PA
CBHW081616220526
45468CB00010B/2904